AMERICAN PRESIDENTS

JOHN F. KENNEDY

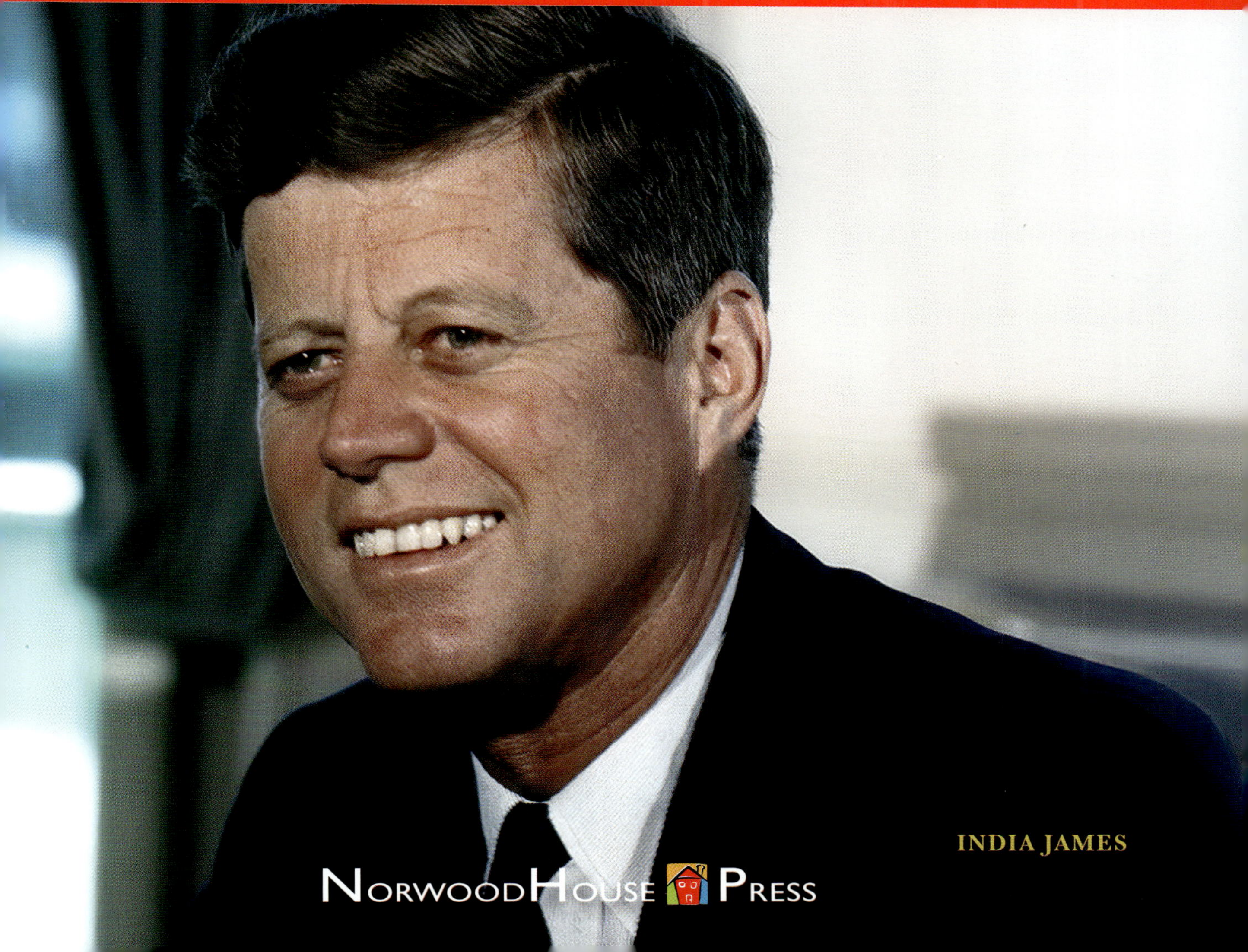

INDIA JAMES

NorwoodHouse Press

Cataloging-in-Publication Data

Names: James, India.
Title: John F. Kennedy / India James.
Description: Buffalo, NY : Norwood House Press, 2027. | Series: American presidents | Includes glossary and index.
Identifiers: ISBN 9781978579903 (pbk.) | ISBN 9781978579910 (library bound) | ISBN 9781978579927 (ebook)
Subjects: LCSH: Kennedy, John F. (John Fitzgerald), 1917-1963--Juvenile literature. | Presidents--United States--Biography--Juvenile literature. | Legislators--United States--Biography--Juvenile literature.
Classification: LCC E842.Z9 J36 2027 | DDC 973.922092--dc23

Published in 2027 by
Norwood House Press
2544 Clinton Street
Buffalo, NY 14224

Designer: Rhea Magaro
Editor: Kim Thompson

Photo credits: Cover, pp. 1, 21 White House; p. 5 Carol M. Highsmith; pp. 6, 8-11, 13-15 Library of Congress; pp. 17, 18 NARA; p. 19 Bettmann;

Printed in the United States of America

Some of the images in this book illustrate individuals who are models. The depictions do not imply actual situations or events.

CPSIA compliance information: Batch #CSNHP27: For further information contact Norwood House Press at 1-800-237-9932.

TABLE OF CONTENTS

Early Years

John Fitzgerald Kennedy was born on May 29, 1917. He lived in this house in Brookline, Massachusetts.

John grew up playing with three brothers and five sisters. Many people called him by the nickname "Jack."

KENNEDY

The family was rich. They spent summers at Hyannis Port on Cape Cod, Massachusetts.

John's father had high expectations. He was very strict. He wanted his children to do great things when they grew up. He hoped that one of them would become president.

Building a Career

John went to Harvard University. After he graduated, he joined the Navy and fought in World War II.

John's ship was destroyed in battle. John was injured, but he managed to pull a wounded crewmate while swimming several miles through the ocean to safety. John was a hero.

When John came home from the war, he became a **politician**. He was elected to **Congress** to represent the state of Massachusetts. He joined the House of Representatives in 1947. He joined the Senate in 1953.

John married Jacqueline "Jackie" Bouvier in 1953.

Presidency

In 1961, John became the 35th president of the United States. He was 43 years old. He holds the record for the youngest person ever to be elected president.

John was president during the **Cold War**. The U.S. and the **Soviet Union** were enemies. Both nations wanted to be the most powerful.

John tried to promote peace. He started the **Peace Corps**. He gave a famous speech in Berlin, Germany. He said he wanted a "peaceful and hopeful globe."

The country was in the middle of the **Space Race**. Both the U.S. and the Soviet Union wanted to be first in space. John supported the U.S. space program. He set a goal for American astronauts to land on the moon.

John hoped to be president for a second **term**. He visited Dallas, Texas, on November 22, 1963. He wanted to ask people there to vote for him.

Sadly, John was **assassinated** in Dallas. He was riding in a car that drove slowly through a crowd when a man with a gun shot him. He died later that day.

Legacy

John F. Kennedy is remembered as a great leader. He was a young president who made difficult decisions for his country. He was a war hero. He made it possible for American astronauts to go to the moon.

Glossary

assassinated (uh-SAS-uh-nay-ted): murdered someone who is well-known or important

Cold War (kohld wor): the period from 1945 to 1991 when the U.S. and the Soviet Union were in conflict but did not fight an actual war with weapons

Congress (CON-gruhs): the part of the U.S. government that makes laws and that includes the House of Representatives and the Senate

Peace Corps (pees kor): an organization of volunteers who help people in poor countries around the world

politician (pah-li-TISH-uhn): a person elected or chosen to hold a government office

Soviet Union (SOH-vee-et YOON-yuhn): a former nation that was divided into several smaller countries in 1991, including Russia and Ukraine

Space Race (spays race): a period from 1955 to 1975 when the United States and the Soviet Union competed to set records for space travel and exploration

term (turm): a definite or set period of time; American presidents are elected to a term that lasts four years

Thinking Questions

1. What state did John represent in Congress?
2. What made John a war hero?
3. Name something John did to promote peace.
4. How did John help America in the Space Race?
5. How did John die?

Index

About the Author

India James writes about science, technology, math, and history for young readers. She loves learning new things while writing books. India lives in Ohio with her family.